Women Inventors

SRA

Columbus, OH

SRAonline.com

 SRA

Send all inquiries to this address:
SRA/McGraw-Hill
4400 Easton Commons
Columbus, OH 43219

ISBN: 978-0-07-608696-2
MHID: 0-07-608696-8

1 2 3 4 5 6 7 8 9 NOR 13 12 11 10 09 08 07

What do the electric lightbulb, the paper clip, and penicillin have in common? They are inventions. Their development came about because someone saw a need for them.

Early humans invented the first tools for the same reasons people invent things today. Using tools makes jobs easier or the world safer. Some inventions are simple time savers. Others are genuine life savers

Many inventors are women. Both women and men notice needs and fill those needs by creating new inventions. Today men and women are likely to invent similar things. But in the past, women sometimes found different needs to fill than men.

3

Until the 1900s it was common for women to work around the home and raise children. Their daily responsibilities may have included farming, food preparation, and teaching children. Women noticed a need for tools to help them in their daily lives, such as the dishwasher and the paper bag.

In the past, women's roles were often different from men's roles. Women were often in caretaking roles. They invented ways to help other people or to make the world safer. Margaret Knight, for example, invented a safety device for looms, which are tools used to make fabric.

1712 Sybilla Masters

The first woman given credit for an invention was Sybilla Masters. She invented a machine for grinding corn. It saved people a lot of time. In the early 1700s all foods were made from scratch. Native Americans had shown settlers how to grow corn. But the corn had to be ground by hand before it could be used to make other foods. Masters was the wife of the mayor of Philadelphia. She went to England to get her invention patented, but the patent had to be in her husband's name. Getting a patent gives the inventor exclusive rights to the invention.

1809 Mary Dixon Kies

Straw bonnets were popular among American women in the early 1800s. Mary Dixon Kies invented a new way to weave straw and thread together to make hats. She took her invention to a hat factory in New England. Her timing was perfect. The United States had just put an embargo on products imported from Europe. That meant that no products could be shipped into this country from Europe. Kies's invention boosted the hat business's sales. In turn, that bettered the New England economy. Kies was the first woman ever to receive a United States patent in her own name.

1812 Tabitha Babbit

If you have ever watched someone work with wood, you have probably seen a saw of some kind. Long ago, all saws were handsaws. To cut down a tree, two people stood at the ends of the saw and moved it back and forth. Tabitha Babbit thought there had to be a better way. She made a thin metal disc, notched it around the edges, and attached it to the spindle of her spinning wheel so it would turn around and around. Thanks to Babbit, circular saws are now used around the world.

1842 Augusta Ada Byron

Where would we be today without computers? Millions of people have at least one of them in their home. Programmers (the people who make the computers work) use a language to move information into computers. This language is like a code. One of the first people to develop this kind of code was Augusta

Ada Byron. She was a mathematician. Many people consider the code she invented to be the first computer program. The code worked so well that the United States Navy named a computer language ADA.

Augusta Ada Byron

1850 Margaret Knight

As a child, Knight loved to tinker with tools, and she got great results. She built mechanical toys for her brothers and a foot warmer for her mother. When she was twelve she saw someone get hurt while working on a loom for making fabric at a local cotton mill. She was certain she could invent something that would prevent more injuries. That very year, she came up with a part for a loom that did just what she intended for it to do. To this day Knight's invention can be found on large looms all over the world.

1871 Margaret Knight

By the time Knight died in 1914 she held twenty-six patents. Although she was not the first woman to invent something, she was one of the busiest. In her time she was called "the female Edison." Knight received patents for things as diverse as clasps for robes and a type of window frame and sash. She even got a patent for a type of rotary engine. The same kind of engine is found on modern jet planes. She is also famous for a practical invention used by millions of people every day.

When Knight was a young woman, paper bags were cone-shaped. They did not hold much and fell apart easily. Knight thought there was a better way to carry groceries and other items. For two years she worked on a machine that would cut the paper and glue the bottom ends together, making the bag able to stand on its own. Someone stole her idea and got the patent for it, but she took him to court and won the case. Knight refused to allow someone else to take credit for her invention.

Sarah Goode invented this space-saving bed.

1885 Sarah Goode

Is your bedroom small and cramped? Wouldn't it be great to figure out a new way to make more space? That's exactly what Sarah Goode did. Goode owned a furniture store in Chicago. She invented a bed that would fold up against a wall, into a cabinet. When the bed was folded up like that, it could be used as a desk. It even had compartments for paper and writing supplies. Goode was the first African American woman to hold a United States patent.

1886 Josephine Cochran

Many homes now have a dishwasher, but it wasn't always so. Josephine Cochran loved to have guests over for meals. She had servants, but they rarely washed dishes fast enough for her, and sometimes they broke the dishes they were washing. So Cochran took matters into her own hands. She invented the first dishwasher and showed it at the World's Fair. The only people who were interested in it, though, were those who owned restaurants and hotels. It took until the 1950s for the home dishwasher to begin to catch on.

Marie Curie

1898 Marie Curie

If you've ever broken a bone, you've probably had an X-ray taken. An X-ray is a way of taking a picture of the bones in your body. Marie Curie was the first person to use X-rays in this way. Curie was a scientist from Poland. She discovered two radioactive elements. One of them, polonium, was named after her birth country. The other was called radium, from the Latin word for *ray*. Curie was the first person ever to win two Nobel Prizes for her work. In honor of Curie and her husband, Pierre, element number 96 was named curium.

1903 Mary Anderson

Let's say you're out with your parents, riding in a car. First it's a drizzly day, and then it begins to rain hard. With a flick of a switch, the windshield wipers come on, clearing the water off the window and making it safe to drive once again. That's a great idea, right? Mary Anderson thought that too. She invented the first set of windshield wipers and received a patent for them. At the time, cars were not enclosed, so you had to reach out and crank the wipers yourself. But one thing led to another, and those original wipers developed into the ones we use today.

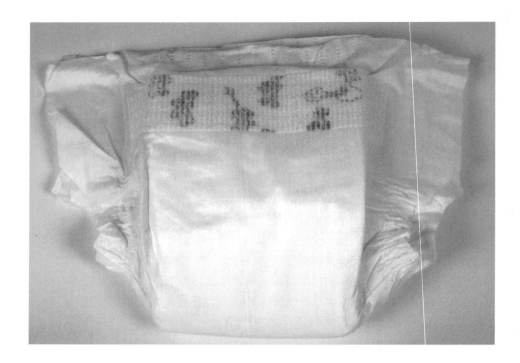

1950 Marion Donovan

There is a saying that necessity is the mother of invention. For Marion Donovan nature's necessity led her to create a protective diaper for her child. Donovan sewed a piece of shower curtain onto the surface of her child's cloth diaper. Her "boaters," as she called them, used snaps instead of pins. They caught on quickly. In later versions, she used parachute fabric to make the diapers. Donovan went on to invent the first real disposable diaper. She started her own company but later sold it. She was paid more than a million dollars for it, which was a good deal of money at the time.

1951 Bessie Nesmith Graham

Bessie Nesmith Graham wanted to be an artist. But when she became a divorced mother, she found work as a secretary. This was before computers. Back then people used typewriters to write letters. There was no way to correct typing mistakes. But the artist inside Graham remembered one of the techniques that painters use when they make mistakes. They paint over them. An idea was born. Graham mixed up a batch of ingredients in her kitchen blender. She created correction fluid. What Graham called "Mistake Out" now comes in little black-and-white bottles and can still be found in practically every office in the country.

1952 Grace Hopper

Remember Augusta Ada Byron's computer code? Grace Hopper, a United States Navy officer, worked with computers. She invented COBOL, a computer language. It is now the most widely used computer language in the entire world. It lets programmers make computers able to talk to each other. You couldn't do most of the things you do on a computer without it. Hopper once found a problem in an early computer and decided that a moth was the cause. The moth had gotten stuck inside. That was the birth of the computer "bug."

1959 Ruth Handler

Once there was a woman who had a daughter named Barbara and a son named Ken. Her daughter enjoyed playing with dolls. While on a family trip to Europe Handler saw a doll that looked like a grown woman. When she returned home, she went to work on an idea. Three years later she exhibited her new doll at the American Toy Fair in New York. The rest, as the saying goes, is history. Can you guess the doll's name?

Ruth Handler

1965 Stephanie Kwolek

School is out. You put on your bike helmet and head for home. You get to your house and go inside. You turn on a television program and watch the police in pursuit of a bad guy. The police have on bulletproof vests. What does any of this have to do with women inventors? Stephanie Kwolek invented the fiber that makes a bulletproof vest bulletproof. It is five times stronger than steel but weighs much less. Although it was originally invented as a lightweight fiber to use for car tires, the fiber is now used in bike helmets and brakes, camping equipment, skis, and dozens of other things too.

1979 Rose Totino

You open the freezer and peer in to find a frozen pizza. Twenty minutes later you're munching on a chewy crust. You're wiping gooey cheese off your chin. Where did this mouthwatering treat originate? Rose Totino and her husband opened a pizza take-out restaurant in Minnesota. People liked the pizza, but they wanted to eat it in the restaurant. So the Totinos added tables and chairs. Years later Totino decided to package the pizza and freeze it so that people could take it home to cook. She made a special kind of crust and got a patent for it.

1712   Sybilla Masters's cornmeal grinder

1776   United States' Independence

1809   Mary Dixon Kies's hat weaver

1812   Tabitha Babbit's circular saw

1842   Augusta Ada Byron's computer code ADA

1850   Margaret Knight's loom safety feature

1861–1865 United States Civil War

1871   Margaret Knight's paper bag

1885   Sarah Goode's pull-down bed

1886 Josephine Cochran's dishwasher

1898 Marie Curie uses X-rays to help people

1903 Mary Anderson's windshield wipers

1919 Nineteenth Amendment to the United States Constitution, stating women's right to vote

1950 Marion Donovan's disposable diapers

1951 Bessie Nesmith Graham's correction fluid

1952 Grace Hopper's COBOL computer code

1959 Ruth Handler's grown-up dolls

1965 Stephanie Kwolek's lightweight fiber that is stronger than steel

1979 Rose Totino's frozen pizza

Vocabulary

genuine (jen´ yə wen) (page 3) *adj.* Real; true.

common (ko´ mən) (page 4) *adj.* Happening often; familiar.

results (ri zults´) (page 9) *n.* Plural form of **result:** What you find out when you do an experiment.

rarely (râr´ lē)(page 13) *adv.* Not often.

drizzly (driz´ ə lē) (page 15) *adj.* Slightly rainy.

techniques (tek neks´) (page 17) *n.* Plural for of **technique:** Method; way of doing things.

pursuit (pûr so͞ot) (page 20) *n.* The act of chasing.

Comprehension Focus: Drawing Conclusions

1. Why would you draw the conclusion that many of the inventions the women in this story made had to do with the home?

2. What information from the story leads you to draw the conclusion that women inventors were not always given credit for their work?